Praise

I am delighted to learn about this collection of poems by Raghav Gupta, a bright young student of fifteen with an expressive mind and a gift for writing. I hope he will keep sharpening his craft, as all writers must, and offer more to us as he grows older and richer in experience. I give Raghav my best wishes for this collection and for his future.

***Dr Shashi Tharoor** - Member of Parliament for Thiruvananthapuram, Chairman of the Parliamentary Standing Committee on External Affairs*

A poet-philosopher even before he is of voting age! Raghav's poems are reflective of a young mind full of ideas about a better world.. May he go from strength to strength

***Rajdeep Sardesai** - Consulting editor India Today Group, Renowned Indian Journalist, Television Anchor and Author.*

Raghav, at just 15 years of age, has a poetic soul that feels ancient. His pains, joys, and doubts derive from the world around him - a world he is observing as keenly as he analyses his inner thoughts. Lines like "it's not poetry, if it's not obscure" & "leave it to poets, to perceive nothingness" speak of his deep engagement with his own art. Reading these poems is like diving into the mind of an aware, self-assured, & insightful young global citizen.

***Varun Grover** - Screenwriter (Masaan),* lyricist *(Gangs of Wasseypur, Ankhon Dekhi, Masaan, Dum Laga Ke Haisha) & standup comedian*

For one so young, Raghav Gupta's poems show a deep introspection of life and all of its flavours. He explores not just life's pleasantries but also its pain and suffering, at both physical and metaphysical plane. I wish him all the best.

***Sh M K Modi** - Renowned Industrialist & Art Connoisseur (MD Modi Industries, Modi Nagar)*

I've known Raghav for many years now. An intelligent student Raghav combines a rare sensitivity in his personality. Raghav comes from a distinguished family which is deeply involved in the warp and weft of school. I was quite amazed and pleased by the depth of emotion in Raghav's poetry.

May his poetry inspire more young people to find similar expression. May the poet in him stay alive and thrive! God bless!

***Aditi Misra** - Principal of DPS, Sector 45, Gurgaon*

Shades of Life

Raghav Gupta

ZORBA BOOKS

Published in India by Zorba Books, 2016

Website: www.zorbabooks.com
Email: info@zorbabooks.com

ISBN Print Book – 978-93-85020-58-2
ISBN eBook – 978-93-85020-59-9

Zorba Books Pvt. Ltd.(opc)

Gurgaon, INDIA

Printed in India

I would like to dedicate this book to
my Parents, Grandparents, Teachers and
friends who have guided and blessed me
in the journey of life.

I would also like to dedicate
this book to the unknown soul-mate
who inspired me to write.

I would also like to thank
each person who has ever been part of
my life in shaping me into "who I am."

Foreword

Poetry has been on the decline in the most of the 20th century. The onset of the digital age, analogues and androids is threatening its existence as a pursuit. Dots and digits and their presumed success in making a global life easy has dulled sensibility and creative imagination.

The younger generation is used to texting and the harshly abbreviated messaging as a mode of instant communication in most of the world caught in a rat race. Leisure is spent in the shopping malls, and food joints and on websites full of fun and games.

But there can always be exceptions in every generation, including in today's young men and women who are keen to follow their passion to what they believe in, or feel, or inclined to think. Raghav Gupta is just 15 years old school student of New Delhi who is trying to feel the value of emotions in human life and the flight of imagination and how they can be woven into poetry.

Whenever he gets time off from heavy syllabus the Indian school education is afflicted with, or some sports or other school activities, he withdraws into himself and dabbles in poetry. The result is his manuscript of a collection of his poems he has written for his proposed website publication, hoping that it will reach a wider audience than he would have got it in a printed publication. He has chosen to make use of the digital age to express his feelings and reflections on life, love, light and darkness, soul and soul-mates. Sometimes he lets his feelings find their own path in imagination and at other times, he lets his mind wonder to the sun and darkness on earth.

Raghav is still young but goes on expressing his feelings and thoughts in poetry. He can emerge as a poet.

My good wishes to him.

H K Dua

Former Editor of the Hindustan Times, Indian Express and the Tribune and the Editorial Advisor of the Times of India.
New Delhi August 29, 2016

Content

Shades of Life

Raghav Gupta

I Pray

I pray
To the God
Who has no colour
No race, no religion
With no *Bible, no Quran,*
And no *Geeta.*
That one day I would
Like to live in a world
Free from poverty
Free from wars, and
Free from prejudice.
And that we homosapiens
Gather around a bonfire
To recite songs written
By the hands of martyrs
On the paper made from
Our heavenly trees.

//Raghav Gupta

Friend

Within you I have found the perfect friend
But someone I know will be there till the end!
And they are not just thoughts I hope will fulfil
Thoughts that will stand forever still.
You have always been unique from the rest
You hold a piece of me no other can possess
My dearest friend, our friendship that was built in a remarkable way
Hope we can keep it, till our hair turns grey
At times I wonder what makes you qualities to stun;
An epitome of sheer beauty, the smile, the trust, or the way you care.
... At times I wonder what makes you fun?
Then I answer myself with a resounding yes;
You are the one person irritating, crying but a gem unwillingly to confess.
You are one of a kind
Oh! Dear friend of mine
I wish the best of everything for you in the world
My many surprises for you unfold....

//Raghav Gupta

The Candescence and The Darkness

The devil
Wanted to buy
My soul using
Currency permeated
In blood.

....I told him
That my soul
Was sold to the highest bidder
Whose name is God.

//Raghav Gupta

Love Addict

I crave love like
Addicts who crave
Their drugs and look
For their next fix
I can't get enough
Of it.

Only this drug
For which I speak
Is a medicinal herb
Imported from the
Exotic garden in
Which love was born.

//Raghav Gupta

The Scarred Soul

The scars look for me
They find solace in my
Bones;
They find solace
In a damaged soul.
Who finds solace in the
Consumption of solemnity?
Wherever the sun sets
Is where the scars go
And I join them too.

//Raghav Gupta

Mindless

I wish that when
I open my eyes
A calm world
Unfolds
Right before me.
Where the lights
Are not so dim
And bouquets
Of blue roses are
In our hands,
Not guns
From which triggers
Are pulled by the cold
Index fingers of hatred.

//Raghav Gupta

Poetry

For heavy, sullen hearts
It's considered a cure.

You may want to embellish it
With aggrandised couture

But remember, it's not poetry
If it's not obscure!

//Raghav Gupta

They Call Me A Mad Child...

They call me a mad child
Because I drink from the
Very soul of insanity.
They call me a Mad child
Because I thrive off every drop
Of life that is wrecked upon my skin, and I let it set fire,
Through my veins and ignite
My blood into a flame of
Drive, lust and desire to achieve
Absolute brilliance.

//Raghav Gupta

Knowledge Leads to Freedom

Our brains
Are locked in
Rusty shackles...

We are prisoners
Of our ignorance.

And knowledge holds
The brass key to our freedom.

//Raghav Gupta

The One

Destiny
Tells us that
We were made
For each other.
If you are indeed
The one......be
My only one
And see how
My unconditional
Love savours
That very moment
When we first
Met.

//Raghav Gupta

The One Tears of Solitude

A man devoid
Of tears is a man
Devoid of a soul.

It is okay to feel as
Though you are
Weak. It is okay to
Weep once in a
Lifetime, if not
All the time,
For tears are the
Bricks used to
Build a man.

//Raghav Gupta

When Darkness Surrounded Me

Words were my
Rays of sunshine
When the dark
Clouds followed
Me everywhere.
I stepped forward
Making me believe
Tomorrow was
Just a mirage

//Raghav Gupta

Our Notes

Our notes
Inscribed with
The thick colours
Of our blood
Create a portal
To another dimension
That is absent from
Prejudice, oppression
Suppression and heartbreak

//Raghav Gupta

Imperfections

She conveyed
To me that
Her imperfections
Could drive me away
From her.
I told her
Our imperfections
Bring us one step
Closer
In these turbulent
Times.

//Raghav Gupta

A True Man

It takes a man
To admit to his
Vulnerabilities and
Take off the mask that
Makes him someone who
He's not...and hides the
Scars etched on the
Core of his face
A true man
Is a man who cries
Even when the world
Tells him not to
.....because he shouldn't

//Raghav Gupta

Love

Love is
The language
Through which
We communicate
To express our respect
And our unbreakable
Link with one another.

Love is
When the universe
Remains intact
When the shooting stars
Fly above us when
They gaze at the bridge
We cross to get
To each other
And spread our wings
...and fly high to the heavens.

Love is
Laughter, joy
Health, peace
Unity, and jubilance.

//Raghav Gupta

Love (Part 2)

Love is
What pumps our
Soft red velvet hearts
At intense speeds and voracity.
When two souls are interwoven
Tightly into strings of musical
Melodies, when they know
They are a match made in heaven.
Love is
Appreciating life,
And rearranging
Its complexities into
Beauty in the form
Of a goddess.

//Raghav Gupta

Love (Part 3)

Love is
The glue that
Holds us together
In times of darkness.

Love is
When we tend
To crying children
Who are left helpless
And were not loved since
Their very first day in the womb.

Love is
Passion, affection
Affinity, strength
Humility and empathy
Fused together to
Form a bouquet of roses.

//Raghav Gupta

Love (Part 4)

Love is not a part time
Thing; it's always there,
When you need it, and
It's always available to
Pick up the phone to
Hear your slurred, sombre
Anecdotal speeches.
When two bottles of
Strong liquor couldn't
Satisfy your needs...

//Raghav Gupta

Lovers

I'm waltzing to the
Rhythm of my heartbeat.
Wobbling from left to right
As the sound of the drums
Spills onto the wooden floor
Of my apartment.
Playing a tune that only
You and I are familiar with.
Dancing as vibrantly as they
Come; Music as luscious
As the tone of your voice
Which flows through my
Ears, and makes its way
Into the song on rotation.
The night is dark
Yet soulful, knowing
That it is just us in
Our lonesomeness, confined
To this dancing and wobbling.

//Raghav Gupta

Serenity

The cure
To my
Misery
Is laughter
I reminisce
About the
Good times
To create a
Mental collage
That shows my
People that
Life is all about
Health and serenity.

//Raghav Gupta

Camouflage

He camouflages
Himself in large bushes
Of inked words,
To walk away
From the black clouds
That follow him
Everywhere he roams.
He tried camouflaging
Himself in big bottles
Of liquor. But the black
Clouds still lingered
Like a dog barking at
Its owner for food.

//Raghav Gupta

Imperfect Relations

I want an imperfect relationship with you.
Yes, imperfect. Because imperfect makes
It real. And when it's real, it's true. And
When it's true, it's good. And when it's
Good, it grows. And when it grows, we'll
Bear fruit. And with fruit comes seeds to
Sow. I would sow my time into you. Make
Words rhyme just for you. Form a life with
Only you. Change the world just like you Do.

//Raghav Gupta

Passion

The smell of your lips
Lingers menacingly
On mine
Like venom it
Gushes through
Every pore and vein.
But it is the only
Antidote I seek.
It is the poison
I'll gladly breathe.

//Raghav Gupta

Soul Mate

No One can tear us apart now
Not even god himself...
Because now we are one unit
With two connected hearts
This love will always be there
Whether you are there or not
This love will keep me alive
And our unbreakable link
With one another
Will remain intact
Till we are left on our funerals.

//Raghav Gupta

Secret of Success

Limitless as the sand,
Softer than a lovers hand,
Deeper than ocean rifts,
Higher than the mountain lifts,
Sweeter than the taste of rain,
Brighter than a golden vein.
Exists existence from within,
Another world beneath the skin,
Broken free of all confines,
Is the stillness of the mind?

//Raghav Gupta

Life

We have been told
Plenty of times
That we must write
Our own stories.
For one day this
Earth we call home
Could disappear and
There will be no one
To tell our stories
And there will be no one
To tell us how
Life in itself is art.

//Raghav Gupta

Visitor of My Dreams

You had visited my dreams
At times when I harboured
You in my mind
Night in and night out.
Welcoming you with
Wide open arms,
The experience of us
Sharing countless of
Cold winter mornings
Together watching the
Snow touch the pavement
All while covered in
Layers of bed comforters.
Was on cloud nine
It all felt real to me and
I knew that if I ever woke up
Then all of those moments
Would wither away...and
That is when I would have
To deal with a reality in which
You are not present....

//Raghav Gupta

Poet's Desire

A pen is the only
Friend you need
It has always been there
When you couldn't pull
The words of our tongue
To let world know you
Were moulded into
Something
Special, even when you
Felt like the sun had seen
Better days, and you weren't
In any of them.

//Raghav Gupta

Musician

He didn't play the
Music, instead the
Music had him on
Its firm grip, playing
Him instead; interlacing
A string of lullabies
That could make any
Living thing waltz
As though the
Euphoria was a cold
Glass of champagne
That sends a soothing
Buzz trickling down
The spine; that feeling
Was the rhythm of the
Music and how much
Love he made to it
Was perhaps left to
The imagination.

//Raghav Gupta

Perceptions, Altercation & Oblivion

I remember when the
Cadences of words gave
Out on deaf ears at
Early dawn; the earth
Stood still, and the
World's mantel clock,
With its TICKING and
TOCKING, counted down
Each second we had left
Before one of us walked
Away into oblivion.

//Raghav Gupta

Portrayal can be Deceptive

He refused to
Look at his world
For what it was
Arming himself with
A gun of which the
Steel was as gelid
As his mind, because
He had no conception
Of what it meant to be
Enraptured by life's
Dulcet bubble; his heart
Was rendered nebulous
With every ring of apathy
And his bones grew
Decrepit.
But underneath it all
He wished everything
Could be different.

//Raghav Gupta

What is A Good Decision?

What is a good decision?
Every decision feels like
a good one at first,
that's why we do it.
Humans aren't designed
to self-vandalise,
so naturally we will choose
what feels right.
We will go with the instinct
that we feel in our gut
that pierces through us
and throbs in our minds.
We fantasize about the best
conclusion
and believe that ours
is the good decision
until we ourselves believe it.
That is when the table turns
and we realise our world
is just an illusion of fancy?
So, who are we to say
What a good decision is?
None of us actually make them.

//Raghav Gupta

Answers

I'll ask her how her
Day was. To which
She will respond with
Her skull resting upon
My shoulders.
And that is all I need
To know; then comes
A kiss that will land
On her forehead.
That will be my answer
And that will be her
Oasis.

//Raghav Gupta

Friendship

You are my best friend, you belong in my heart.
We go through ups and downs, even then nothing can tear us apart.
I see you as my best friend...and I'll always care
Love, respect and trust are the things we share.
I know you as a person, and especially as a friend,
Our friendship is something that will never end.
My friendship with you is special and true,
When we are together we stick like glue.
When I'm in the darkness and need some light,
I know things will turn out right when you are by my side.
Our friendship is so strong, it breaks down bars,
And shines bright like the sun and stars.
I met you as a stranger, took you as a friend
I hope our long friendship never ends.
It is like a magnet, our friendship, pulling us together,
Because no matter where we are,
Our friendship will last forever.

//Raghav Gupta

Some Demons and A Whisky

The demons were the
monkeys on his back.
And thinking that
Pouring more of his
Whisky would
Make them leap right off
The epiphany that never
Made its way into his brain.
Was that the demons wanted
Him to keep pouring more of
That liquor....after all,
Who brewed that whisky?

//Raghav Gupta

Ordinary Man

In my present life,
I'm just an ordinary man
With too little to give
And too much too lose;
In my past life
I was a poet who recited
Songs that were tattooed
Into my silky skin, and the
Ink submerged into my
Bloodstream wrote more
Songs for the ordinary man
In me to vocalise to a crowd
Of aching strangers...

//Raghav Gupta

Puppet of Love

Her eyes can be
Piercing
But no matter
What surfaces from
Underneath
She knows that she
Is under cupid's spell
With strings tightly
Attached to the
Circumference of her heart.
She knows as much
As I do that Cupid
It will only bring me
Closer to her; because
He's the puppet master of this thing we call love.

//Raghav Gupta

The Darker Side

I don't t see darkness
As this place with no
Visible light; rather it
Is a pistol that could be
Attached to a person's
Hand when they feel
Like the cracks in their
Walls can't be repaired
Or when that day comes
When they feel like the
Only way to drift apart
From such a confusing
World is to swallow more
Pills and drown in a
Deep pool of filthy vodka;
When everything that is
Artistic about beautiful
Children is wiped away
From our memories; or
When that day comes
When our voice becomes
Silent and there are no
More poems to fill our

Blank pages; that's the
True face of darkness
And it's eerie complexion...

//Raghav Gupta

Drapes of Lies

There's a reason they don't
Tell you the truth.
There's a reason they wrap
You up in drapes of lies.
Because they are afraid that
You'll make it out alive.
Because they don't know you're the
Unscratched truth and you'll
Skin the lies alive.

//Raghav Gupta

Poet

Leave it to poets
To perceive nothingness
As an unattainable
Spark of light and
Turn it into something
It starts with thin white
Sheets of paper and
A stroke of a pen
To summon life into
Their own world.

//Raghav Gupta

Nature

Flux of freshwater
Runs deep in my skin.
The wind's gust paddles our
Fingers closely
Into a clutch
As we bathe in
The sun's ray
And dab our moisten flesh
In the pasty cotton clouds.

//Raghav Gupta

God

I have inhaled you.
I can feel you behind my eyes.
You have gotten into my bloodstream.
I can feel u flowing in me.

//Raghav Gupta

Life

They tell me life is A rollercoaster,
But sometimes I feel like I was
Denied tickets at the front gate.
And I've been forced to enjoy
The ride from outside ever since.

//Raghav Gupta

Dream

In this dream I had
Conceived, I took you
By your palms. Surveyed
Them with my dark
Brown coffee eyes,
And saw the many wars
You've fought in
How they left you
Begging on your knees
When the last blood you
Spilled fell beneath the
Cracks, and how your
Brittle skin no longer
Couldn't sustain itself
To keep you tucked in
On sleepless frigid nights.

//Raghav Gupta

Sorrow

And each cold night
He picks splinters
From his palms, on
Which the creases are
Outlined with blood.
He has no more love
Left to give to the
Moon, and no more
Virtues to be extolled.
He is a broken man with
Bits and pieces of him
That once moulded him
Into a cosmic star.
He leaves his cluttered
Bed undone, and lies
In it, in the dimly lit
Room with all of his
Sorrows lying next
To him.

//Raghav Gupta

Curiosity

We're just curious souls
Trying to figure out how
Our mind and body works
With every meeting of our lips
That lulls us to a dream
State in which we see
Roses hovering over us
And every rapid heartbeat
At irregular time intervals.

//Raghav Gupta

Love will Hold Me Here

I will always believe in love.
Whether you live it or not. I
Will. It was love that brought
Me here, it will be love that will
Keep me here.
While you run into the
Darkness of money, I'll remain
Here, ready to wind you back
Into light.

//Raghav Gupta

Imagination

I walked the
Cold streets
In December,
Not knowing
Who she was,
And wondering
If she was just
Another locked
Door waiting to
Be busted open.
I thought the
Graffiti on the
Brick walls said
Her name, but it
Was just another
Poem.

//Raghav Gupta

Benevolence

When a light shines,
It does not decide,
By giving favour to beauty,
Over things that wish to hide.

It radiates on all
Illuminating from its source
All things it can, it touches,
Without a glimmer of remorse.

Shadows maybe cast,
As their nature is to show
That a thing has been lit,
By a glorious glow.

//Raghav Gupta

About the Author

The author, Raghav Gupta, is a young 15-year-old boy who on the face of it, has traits that any normal teenager would have. He is cheeky, full of life, humorous and does not give an inkling of the deep thought and emotions that is portrayed in his Poetry, in any other manner.

He is a keen sportsman and an affable young lad who is engaged in educational pursuit like any one his age. He is academically adept and gave his family a surprise by standing 2 nd in the country and 6 thin the world in the English Olympiad exam as much as he surprised them by his poetry.

He wrote these poems over a period of one year quietly even without telling his family about it. He comes from an eminent family of Engineers and Doctors where, like in any other middle class family, creativity is not cherished as a virtue but is just good to have. He wrote the poems on his own accord without any motivation or encouragement.

The work is thus unique and surprises many of his elders, peers and teachers by the sheer depth of emotions which are quite unthinkable from a child of his age. The depth of thinking displayed is not only remarkable, it inspires awe from the way he has meandered into different aspects of life. The Poems portray a deep understanding of the "Shades of Life" at this very young age.

Each of his poems stirs up a storm in the reader and forces the reader to have a world view which is different, unique.

Citations, Awards and Recognition

1. Recipient of Blue Tie for continued academic excellence. This Blue Tie is awarded by Delhi Public School to students who have consistently been awarded the Scholar Batch for 7 consecutive years, for overall academic excellence.

2. Recipient of Blue Blazer. This Blue Blazer is awarded by Delhi Public School to Students who have consistently been awarded Scholar Batch for 3 consecutive years for overall academic excellence.

3. Stood 2nd in India and 6th globally in International English Olympiad Exam

4. Stood 2nd in school in International Maths Olympiad in Class IX

5. Represented school in Dramatics, Basketball, Table – Tennis, Cricket and Badminton in different interschool and district level competitions.

6. Part of Indian Cancer Society and helps spread awareness through 'Nukkad Nataks'.